The essential Disney idea book

Featuring magical scrapbooking and crafting ideas!

ISBN 1-55376-576-1

Printed in Canada

contents

introduction

Whether it's a trip to a Disney theme park, an afternoon of dress-up and make-believe, a favorite bedtime story or a cherished stuffed pal, Disney touches our lives in many wonderful, magical ways.

There may be no greater gift than capturing those special moments today and having them to share with family and friends in the years to come. Sandylion has created an exceptional range of scrapbook stickers, papers, albums and frames to showcase those memories.

This idea book provides over 125 finished project suggestions and countless product ideas extending well beyond traditional memory keeping. Page after page, this book will inspire you, it will make you smile and it will open your eyes and hearts to the wonderful world of Disney.

May all of your memories be magical!

Size: 12" x 12"

Countdown to Disney

by Kathy Fesmire

Supplies:

*Stickers: Mickey, Mickey Borders, Mickey Alphabet,
Embossed Die-cuts: Mickey Names, Rub-on Transfers:
Pooh, Paper: Mickey Ears, Extras: cardstock, buttons,
ribbon, distressing ink, embroidery thread*

Tip:

*Decorated vellum pockets are the perfect way to hold
each of the countdown tags. The gingham ribbon adds
color and texture while it hides the adhesive used to
form the pockets.*

Size: 12" x 12"

A Meeting with Mickey Mouse

by Trudy Sigurdson

Supplies:

Stickers: Mickey, Mickey Borders, Mickey Alphabet, Cardstock Stickers: Mickey Alphabet Ears, Paper: Mickey - Black, Extras: cardstock

Tip:

Don't shy away from enlarging photos and cropping them if needed.

Memories that will last a lifetime

Size: 12" x 12"

Mickey Mouse and Friends

by Trudy Sigurdson

Supplies:

Stickers: Mickey Phrases, Mickey Alphabet, Rub-on Transfers: Mickey, Paper: Mickey - Cobblestone, Extras: cardstock, ribbon, buttons, foam squares

Disney Greetings

by Trudy Sigurdson

Why not create a few cards before your adventure begins and send them to friends and family from the park.

Supplies:

Having Fun with Minnie
Stickers: Mickey Alphabet - Red, Mickey Alphabet, Embossed Die-cuts: Minnie, Paper: Minnie Mouse & Dots, Extras: cardstock

Smile and Say "Mickey"
Stickers: Mickey Phrases, Embossed Die-cuts: Mickey, Paper: Mickey - Black, Extras: cardstock, foam squares

Greetings from the Best Place in the World
Stickers: Mickey Phrases, Embossed Die-cuts: Minnie, Paper: Minnie Mouse & Dots, Extras: cardstock, rubber stamp

A Trip to Remember
Stickers: Mickey Phrases, Embossed Stickers: Pooh, Paper: Pooh Name, Extras: cardstock, ribbon

Yippee! Wow! Cool!
Stickers: Mickey Phrases, Embossed Die-cuts: Mickey, Paper: Mickey Name, Extras: cardstock

Our Disney Journal

by Shannon Lavigne

What better way to start your holiday than to have a journal to record all the wonderful events of your days at the most magical place on earth!

Supplies:
Stickers: Mickey Sketchbook, Mickey Alphabet - Yellow, Bits of Glitz Stickers: Mickey, Papers: Mickey - Black, Mickey Cream Comic, Mickey Name, Minnie Name, Extras: blank journal, rub-ons, glass beads, embossed label, bookplate, stencil, brads, ribbon, dimensional glaze

Tip:
You can buy a plain covered journal and personalize it just the way you want.

Mickey and the Gang

On November 18, 1928, Mickey Mouse made his screen debut in the first sound cartoon "Steamboat Willie". A star was born! Mickey Mouse is one of the most universal symbols of our time. He is a born leader. He is adventurous, enthusiastic, independent, humble and a positive thinker. He is dependable and always looks on the bright side.

"I hope we never lose sight of one fact.. that this was all started by a Mouse." -Walt Disney

Minnie Mouse
Sweet
Fun-Loving
Charming
Gracious

Goofy
Clumsy
Endearing
Dreamer
Innocent

Donald Duck
Outspoken
Impatient
Sore Loser
Hotheaded

Pluto
Curious
Devoted
Faithful
Playful

I had taken a similar photo as this of Aysha with a bunch of Poohs at Disneyland Park and Alex always thought it looked cool. So when we were in Harrod's in London and he saw a big pile of Mickeys, he wanted me to do the same thing with him.
March 2004

MICKEY
and Alex at Harrod's

Size: 12" x 12"

Mickey and Alex
by Trudy Sigurdson

Supplies:
Embossed Stickers: Mickey, Embossed Die-cuts: Mickey Names, Papers: Mickey Tonal, Mickey Name, Extras: cardstock, ribbon, buttons, brads

Tip:
The Mickey title comes alive with the addition of Mickey's ears, arms and gloves. You may want to cut stickers apart to create a personal touch.

An afternoon in the sun

A Trip to Remember

by Yvonne Verdonk

Supplies:

*Stickers: Mickey Travel, Mickey Phrases,
Paper: Travel - Sand, Extras: cardstock, twine, string*

Tip:

*Standard staples and ink helps to create a vintage pocket
envelope perfect to hold both journaling and mementos
from a recent vacation.*

Our vacation

Disney Road Trip '04

by Yvonne Verdonk

Supplies:

*Stickers: Mickey Travel, Mickey
Travel Alphabet, Travel Borders,
Papers: Travel - Sand, Travel -
Clouds, Extras: cardstock*

Tip:

*Like your child's favorite storybook, you can create interest by
having moving parts. The Mickey surfing image is secured on a
moveable strip and fed through a long horizontal slit. When you
pull the tab, Mickey looks like he is surfing through the waves.*

Size: 8" x 8"

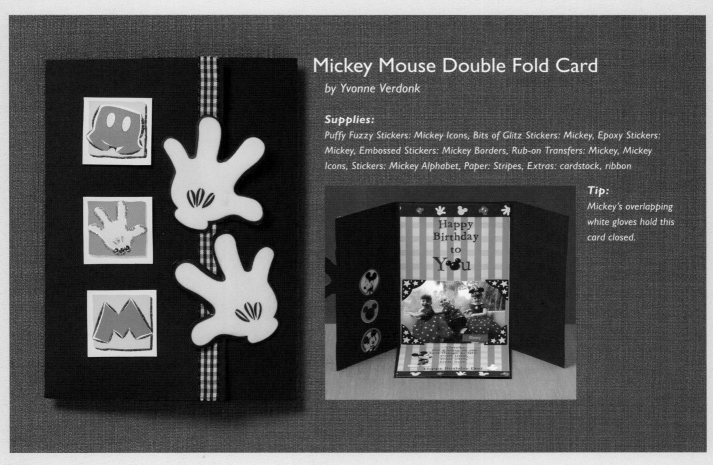

Mickey Mouse Double Fold Card
by Yvonne Verdonk

Supplies:
Puffy Fuzzy Stickers: Mickey Icons, Bits of Glitz Stickers: Mickey, Epoxy Stickers: Mickey, Embossed Stickers: Mickey Borders, Rub-on Transfers: Mickey, Mickey Icons, Stickers: Mickey Alphabet, Paper: Stripes, Extras: cardstock, ribbon

Tip:
Mickey's overlapping white gloves hold this card closed.

Having a good time, just doing my thing

Size: 12" x 12"

Lounging with Mickey
by Cheryl Souter

Supplies:
Epoxy Stickers: Mickey, Stickers: Mickey Phrases, Papers: Dots & Stripes, Mickey - Black, Mickey Name, Extras: cardstock, brads, eyelets, ribbon, distressing ink, staples, elastics

Happily ever after...

Magical Memories

by Yvonne Verdonk

Supplies:

Stickers: Mickey Snapshots, Mickey Phrases, Rub-on Transfers: Mickey, Minnie, Papers: Mickey Tonal, Minnie Tonal, Mickey Name, Minnie Name, Extras: cardboard, black envelopes, ribbon, embroidery thread, jump rings, charms

Tip:

Each pocket or envelope is attached to the previous pocket using the flap. The gummed edge is not strong enough to hold so another adhesive should be used. "He said...", "She said..." is a great way to journal two different perspectives.

Surprise

Top Secret Surprise

by Yvonne Verdonk

Supplies:

Embossed Stickers: Mickey, Mickey Borders, Stickers: Mickey Alphabet, Rub-on Transfers: Mickey, Extras: cardstock, beaded chain, eyelets, buckle, tag, rub-ons

Tip:

This portfolio opens up with a surprise pop-up. It is made by folding a 5" x 10" strip of paper in half. Taking each of the bottom corners, fold the paper up so that each of the bottom corners meets each other at the top of the center fold line. Secure the open back to the center of the portfolio. Open and close the card to reveal and activate the pop-up.

Make a Wish!
by Shannon Lavigne

Supplies:
Embossed Paper Die-cuts: Mickey, Papers: Mickey - Cobblestone, Mickey Poses, Extras: cardstock, ribbon

Tip:
Instead of a standard card, why not make a tri-fold tag? It's like doing 3 mini pages.

Tag Card

Size: 8" x 8"

Mickey Girl
by Beth Leonard

Supplies:
Stickers: Mickey Phrases, Mickey Vintage Comic, Paper: Mickey - Black, Mickey Name, Extras: cardstock, ribbon, eyelets, safety pins, brads, ribbon

Tip:
Simple folded envelopes are made by adhering two patterned papers together before cutting and folding so that they are as beautiful on the inside as they are on the outside.

16

What's cooking Mickey?

Size: 12" x 12"

Say Cheese

by Shannon Lavigne

Supplies:
Stickers: Mickey, Mickey Alphabet - Red, Papers: Mickey
- Cobblestone, Mickey Poses, Mickey - Black, Extras:
cardstock, vellum, eyelets, brads, bookplate, ribbon

Tip:
A gum wrapper braid is a great embellishment and a
great way to use up your scrap paper.

Mickey Mouse Autograph Book

by Shannon Lavigne

Autograph books are a must have when visiting the parks.

Supplies:
Puffy Fuzzy Stickers: Mickey Image, Mickey Icons, Papers: Mickey - Black, Mickey - Cobblestone, Mickey Poses, Extras: cardboard, carabiner, coil binding

It All Started With a Mouse

by Cheryl Souter

Supplies:
Rub-on Transfers: Mickey, Stickers: Mickey Phrases, Paper: Mickey - Cobblestone, Mickey Name, Extras: cardstock, vellum, embossing powder, brads, eyelet, ribbon, distressing ink

Always look on the bright side!

Happiness Is…

by Shannon Lavigne

Supplies:
Stickers: Mickey Geometric, Rub-on Transfers: Mickey, Papers: Mickey Geometric Squares, Mickey Stripes, Extras: cardstock, vellum, bookplate, brads

Size: 12" x 12"

Corey, Khala, & Braydon in Disneyland Park

August 2000

Size: 12" x 12"

Minnie Mouse

by Cheryl Souter

Supplies:
Papers: Dots & Stripes, Red Polka Dot, Embossed
Stickers: Minnie, Minnie Borders, Extras: cardstock,
metal rimmed tags, vellum, brads, ribbon, eyelets,
washers

Tip:
Dimension and texture are added to this layout by
layering the stickers on the metal rimmed tags. Stickers
were first placed on the tags and then the excess was cut
away and positioned under the tag.

Girls will be girls thank goodness

Easy to make and fun to decorate. These purses are great as cards, invitations or for a child's party activity.

Charming

Simply Spots Minnie Purse
by Shannon Lavigne

Supplies:
Rub-on Transfers: Minnie Icons, Paper: Red Polka Dots, Extras: cardstock, jump rings, brads, ribbon, adhesive tab

Just Minnie Purse
by Shannon Lavigne

Supplies:
Rub-on Transfers: Minnie, Minnie Icons, Embossed Die-cuts: Minnie, Papers: Dots & Stripes, Minnie Name, Extras: cardstock, distressing ink, foam squares, ribbon, brads

I think that every child instinctively loves Mickey and Minnie Mouse. It's just part of being a little kid and that is why Disneyland Park is such a magical place for them. So when Aysha and Alex saw Minnie Mouse, they were so excited and had to go and see her. Disneyland Park. September 1997.

Aren't you sweet!

Minnie
by Trudy Sigurdson

Supplies:
Embossed Die-cuts: Mickey Names, Minnie, Paper: Minnie Name, Extras: cardstock

Size: 12" x 12"

Our Minnie

by Shannon Lavigne

Size: 8" x 8"

Supplies:

Stickers: Mickey Snapshots, Papers: Mickey - Black, Minnie Name, Extras: cardstock, vellum, ribbon, brads, distressing ink

Tip:

Find your favorite photo and have it enlarged. Make it a feature page.

Boo Boo Box

by Shannon Lavigne

Supplies:

Embossed Die-cuts: Minnie, Epoxy Stickers: Minnie, Papers: Dots & Stripes, Minnie Name, Extras: cardstock, paint, distressing ink, foam squares, buttons

Tip:

A bandage tin was painted red and then distressed. Paper was layered and then wrapped around the tin.

Our Little Movie Star

by Yvonne Verdonk

Size: 8" x 8"

Supplies:

Rub-on Transfers: Minnie, Minnie Icons, Epoxy Stickers: Minnie, Papers: Red Polka Dots, Dots & Stripes, Extras: cardstock, ribbon, vellum, eyelets, distressing ink

Tip:

Rub-ons are an excellent way to add accents to ribbons, vellum and photos.

Size: 12" x 12"

Girlfriends

Meetin' Minnie
by Shannon Lavigne

Supplies:
Cardstock Stickers: Minnie Mouse, Rub-on Transfers:
Minnie, Minnie Icons, Papers: Yellow Burlap, Extras:
cardstock, ribbon

Minnie Birthday Gift

by Yvonne Verdonk

Supplies:

Embossed Stickers: Minnie, Minnie Borders, Embossed
Die-cuts: Minnie, Paper: Red Polka Dots, Minnie Name,
Extras: cardstock, eyelets, brads, ribbon

Tip:

This box is made with two pieces of 12" x 12" cardstock.
The base is carefully folded as shown below.
Crease the cardstock using a folding blade into nine
4" x 4" squares. The corner squares are also creased
on the diagonal so that they can fold into the center of
the box. The lid is made using the same technique and
secured with glue and eyelets.

Caring is in the little things!

Size: 12" x 12"

Goofy

Gawrsh!

Goofy Card and Tag
by Gigi Tung

Supplies - Card:
Paper: Goofy Tonal, Epoxy Stickers: Goofy, Extras: corrugated cardboard, clasps, twine

Supplies - Tag:
Embossed Die-cuts: Mickey Names, Epoxy Stickers: Goofy, Extras: corrugated cardboard, ribbon, brads

Tip:
The corrugated cardboard used for the card was painted and then sanded for a distressed look.

Goofy's Kitchen
by Cheryl Souter

Size: 8" x 8"

Supplies:
Paper: Goofy Tonal, Embossed Die-cuts: Mickey Names, Frame Kit: Goofy, Epoxy Stickers: Goofy, Extras: cardstock, envelope, vellum, ribbon, clip

Tip:
You don't always have to use a whole frame or even use it as a frame at all. A corner of the Goofy frame was ripped to add a punch of striped color to the top left hand corner.

Oops, goofed again!

Size: 12" x 12"

You're So Goofy
by Shannon Lavigne

Supplies:
Stickers: Goofy, Extras: cardstock, bookplate, embroidery thread, fibres, brads

24

Happy Birthday Pocket Card

by Yvonne Verdonk

Supplies:

Stickers: Donald, Donald Borders, Mickey Phrases, Mickey Alphabet - Yellow, Extras: cardstock

Tip:

Sticker words and letters are great when combined with your computer journaling. When combining text and stickers remember you may need to adjust your font's character spacing as well as your line spacing.

Donald

You quack me up!

Aysha Meets Donald

by Trudy Sigurdson

Supplies:

Stickers: Donald, Donald Borders, Mickey Alphabet - Red, Embossed Die-cuts: Mickey Names, Extras: cardstock

Tip:

Panoramic photos are a great way to get "the whole shot" without lots of extra.

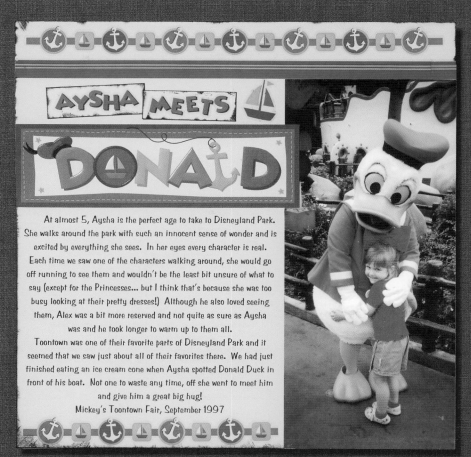

At almost 5, Aysha is the perfect age to take to Disneyland Park. She walks around the park with such an innocent sense of wonder and is excited by everything she sees. In her eyes every character is real. Each time we saw one of the characters walking around, she would go off running to see them and wouldn't be the least bit unsure of what to say (except for the Princesses... but I think that's because she was too busy looking at their pretty dresses!) Although he also loved seeing them, Alex was a bit more reserved and not quite as sure as Aysha was and he took longer to warm up to them all. Toontown was one of their favorite parts of Disneyland Park and it seemed that we saw just about all of their favorites there. We had just finished eating an ice cream cone when Aysha spotted Donald Duck in front of his boat. Not one to waste any time, off she went to meet him and give him a great big hug! Mickey's Toontown Fair, September 1997

Size: 12" x 12"

Pluto Matchbook Tag

by Yvonne Verdonk

Supplies:

Stickers: Pluto, Pluto Borders, Travel Borders, Papers: Travel - Clouds, Mickey Name, Extras: cardstock, ribbon, staples

Tip:

Just like an original matchbook, colorful staples are an ideal way to secure the left fold of this Pluto tag.

Size: 8" x 8"

Hangin' Out with Pluto

by Trudy Sigurdson

Hanging out with Pluto!
Disneyland Park, December 2003

Supplies:

Stickers: Pluto, Pluto Borders, Extras: cardstock, foam squares

Tip:

One large photo is often more effective than three or four small photos.

Pluto Tag

by Gigi Tung

Supplies:

Stickers: Pluto, Paper: Mickey - Cobblestone, Toy Story Green, Extras: cardstock, metal rimmed tags, twill ribbon, jump ring, brads, distressing ink

Tip:

Layering smaller tags gives you the option to add other elements that relate to the character.

Mickey Mouse Tag
by Cheryl Souter

Supplies:

Stickers: Mickey Sketchbook, Mickey Alphabet - Red, Puffy Fuzzy Stickers: Mickey Icons, Papers: Mickey Poses, Mickey Tonal, Mickey Name, Extras: cardstock, ribbon, slide mount, pocket-size CD

The Gang

Do you believe in magic?

Size: 12" x 12"

Autographs from Disneyland Park
by Cheryl Souter

Supplies:

Embossed Die-cuts: Mickey Names, Stickers: Mickey Sketchbook, Papers: Mickey - Black, Mickey Poses, Disney - Cobblestone, Mickey Red Comic, Mickey Cream Comic, Extras: cardstock, distressing ink, silver string, photo turns, brads, washers, embossed label, dimensional glaze

Our Vacation Video

by Shannon Lavigne

Supplies:
Stickers: Mickey Snapshots, Papers: Mickey - Black, Mickey Name, Minnie Name, Extras: vellum, ribbon, embroidery thread, embossed label, bookplate, brads, beads, ribbon

Tip:
The sticker of Mickey and Minnie has been sanded with sandpaper to give it a muted tone to match the paper. Minnie's polka dots are accented with glass beads.

Character Coasters and Tin

by Shannon Lavigne

Supplies - Tin:
Stickers: Mickey Sketchbook, Papers: Mickey - Black, Mickey Name, Minnie Name, Extras: distressing ink, foam squares

Supplies - Coasters:
Stickers: Mickey Sketchbook, Papers: Mickey - Black, Travel - Clouds, Mickey Name, Minnie Name, Mickey Red Comic, Extras: cardboard

Tip:
Coasters are a unique gift to give to someone who has just been on a Disney vacation or loves Disney. These coasters are fun and easy to make, and the tin is the perfect case for storing them.

This kit contains:
Sunscreen — for the sunshine weather
Extra Film — for all those "gotta have" shots
Kleenex — to dry the tears when you have to leave
Candy — to munch on while waiting in line
Autograph Book — gotta have one of those
Pens — for all those autographs
Bandaids — for the blisters you're sure to get because you just won't want to leave!
Info Info & more info — lots of stuff you need to know about how to get to where you want to go
And most of all...
Best wishes and happy holidays!!
Craig, Shannon, Sterling and Kaeden

Disney Survival Kit

by Shannon Lavigne

Supplies:
Stickers: Mickey Sketchbook, Papers: Mickey Poses, Mickey - Black, Mickey - Cobblestone, Mickey Red Comic, Extras: vellum, foam squares, ribbon

Tip:
The empty paint can was bought at a hardware store. Various patterned papers were cut to size and then adhered together to form one long strip of paper. The strip was then wrapped around the empty paint can. Fill the can with sunscreen, extra film, tickets, etc.

Size: 8" x 8"

It all started with a mouse

Walt and Mickey Mouse

by Trudy Sigurdson

Supplies:
Stickers: Mickey Sketchbook, Papers: Mickey Red Comic, Mickey Cream Comic, Extras: cardstock, foam squares, metal washers, brads, photo corners, distressing ink, ribbon, dimensional glaze

Vintage
Mickey Mouse Mini Tag Book
by Yvonne Verdonk

Supplies:
Stickers: Mickey Sketchbook, Papers: Mickey Red Comic, Mickey Taupe Comic, Extras: cardboard, cardstock, ribbon, distressing ink

Tip:
This mini album is perfect when a little gift memento is needed. Use lightweight cardboard to form the covers.

Mickey Mouse Double Tag

by Gigi Tung

Supplies:

Stickers: Mickey Vintage Comic, Mickey Vintage Comic Accents, Papers: Mickey Cream Comic, Mickey Red Comic, Extras: cardstock, paper bags, tabs, twine, distressing ink, ribbon, foam squares, bookplate, rub-ons

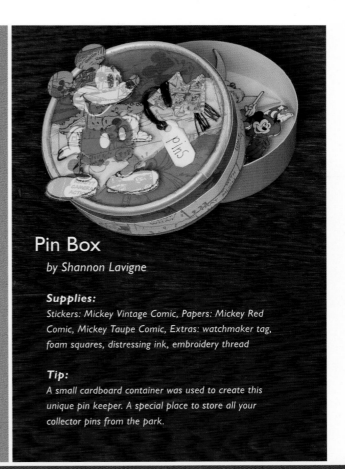

Pin Box

by Shannon Lavigne

Supplies:

Stickers: Mickey Vintage Comic, Papers: Mickey Red Comic, Mickey Taupe Comic, Extras: watchmaker tag, foam squares, distressing ink, embroidery thread

Tip:

A small cardboard container was used to create this unique pin keeper. A special place to store all your collector pins from the park.

Vintage Mickey Mouse

by Beth Leonard

Size: 12" x 12"

Supplies:

Stickers: Mickey Vintage Comic, Mickey Vintage Comic Accents, Papers: Mickey Red Comic, Mickey Cream Comic, Mickey Taupe Comic, Extras: cardstock, vellum, distressing ink, foam squares, ribbon, embossed labels, beaded chain

Tip:

To hand cut great letters, you can print computer text as a mirror image on the back of your favorite patterned paper. This was done to create the word Vintage.

Altered Book

Mickey's Altered Book

by Yvonne Verdonk

Supplies:

Embossed Die-cuts: Mickey, Stickers: Mickey Sketchbook, Mickey Vintage Comic, Mickey Vintage Comic Accents, Mickey Phrases, Pooh Watercolor Accents, Rub-on Transfers: Minnie, Minnie Icons, Mickey, Mickey Icons, Papers: Mickey Stripes, Mickey & Stripes, Mickey - Black, Mickey Travel - Sand, Mickey Name, Mickey Red Comic, Mickey Cream Comic, Mickey Taupe Comic, Extras: cardboard, coil binding, cardstock, ribbon, fibres, transparencies, vellum, distressing ink, safety pin, string, brads, beaded chain, key, keyhole charm

Tip:

This unique double spined book was constructed by hand from lightweight cardboard. Each page opens up like a puzzle to reveal the next secret. The pages are cut off-center altering from the left and right. When you reach the back cover the final treasure is a special envelope which opens up and holds six more photos.

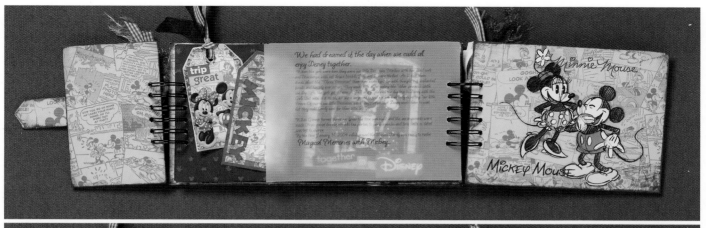

Princesses

They live in worlds of magic and make-believe and fairy tales and happy endings. They are the enchanting Disney Princesses. Whether it is the insatiable curiosity of Ariel, the feisty determination of Tinker Bell or the romantic spirit of Cinderella, each Princess, with her undisputed beauty and grace, has unique qualities that empower her to reach her dreams. The Princesses hold a special place in the hearts and minds of little girls everywhere. Believe in your dreams.

Cinderella
Gentle
Positive
Hardworking
Well-meaning

Snow White
Sweet
Graceful
Gentle
Naive

Ariel
Confident
Curious
Feisty
Headstrong

Belle
Loyal
Intelligent
Adventurous
Stubborn

Aurora
Romantic
Innocent
Gentle
Thoughtful

Jasmine
Curious
Romantic
Dreamer
Adventurous

Tinker Bell
Playful
Jealous
Good-hearted
Feisty

Size: 12" x 12"

Once Upon a Time

by Shannon Lavigne

Supplies:
Stickers: Cinderella, Papers: Cinderella Image, Cinderella Corner, Cinderella Tonal, Cinderella Name, Extras: cardstock, slide mounts, vellum, ribbon, eyelets

Tip:
Don't forget to capture everyday moments.

My Diary

by Shannon Lavigne

Making a beautiful diary for a young girl is a wonderful gift. Personalize it, suiting her personality and interests. There is nothing more fun than designing one of these altered books. Keep adding to it until you get it just the way you want it.

Supplies:

Stickers: Princesses, Princess Phrases, Epoxy Stickers: Cinderella, Bits of Glitz Stickers: Cinderella, Papers: Cinderella Image, Cinderella Name, Cinderella Tonal, Extras: notebook, cardstock, ribbon, fibres, brads

Beautiful as a dream come true

Cinderella Wishes Tag Card

by Yvonne Verdonk

Supplies:

Embossed Die-cuts: Cinderella, Paper: Cinderella Name, Rub-on Transfers: Cinderella, Extras: cardstock, distressing ink, thread, ribbon, eyelets

Tip:

Each of the removable tags are a wonderful place for journaling or writing personal messages.

Your carriage is ready

Size: 8" x 8"

Off to the Ball

by Shannon Lavigne

Supplies:

Stickers: Cinderella Wedding Stickers, Paper: Cinderella - Pink, Princess Tonal Paper: Cinderella, Extras: cardstock, vellum, ribbon, fibres, charms, page pebble, eyelets

Our Dream Come True
by Shannon Lavigne

Supplies:
*Embossed Die-cuts: Cinderella, Paper:
Cinderella - Pink, Cinderella Name,
Extras: cardstock, vellum, brads, distressing ink*

Size: 12" x 12"

Precious

Fairy tales
do come true

Cinderella
by Yvonne Verdonk

Supplies:
*Papers: Cinderella Tonal, Cinderella Name,
Extras: cardstock, glitter, foam squares,
distressing ink*

Tip:
*Add text and titles to your digital photos
before printing.*

Size: 12" x 12"

Cinderella Tag

by Cheryl Souter

Supplies:

Stickers: Cinderella, Papers: Cinderella Name, Cinderella Tonal, Extras: cardstock, ribbon, brads, eyelet, distressing ink, embossing powder, bead

Princess Tags

by Trudy Sigurdson

Supplies:

Stickers: Princess Snapshots, Cinderella, Cinderella Borders, Cinderella Alphabet, Snow White, Snow White Borders, Paper: Snow White Corner, Purple Blend, Extras: cardstock, ribbon, eyelets, lace, foam squares

Fairest of them all

A Visit with Snow White

by Trudy Sigurdson

Supplies:

Stickers: Snow White, Papers: Snow White Image, Snow White Corner, Extras: cardstock, cotton lace, foam squares

Tip:

Applying stickers to cardstock and cutting them out leaving a border, gives them strength so that you can add foam squares for added dimension.

Size: 12" x 12"

Ariel

The Little Mermaid Tag

by Gigi Tung

Supplies:

Stickers: Little Mermaid, Epoxy Stickers: Ariel, Rub-on Transfers: Ariel, Paper: Ariel Tonal, Extras: cardstock, fibres, brad, foam squares

Tip:

Epoxy stickers have a clear dome on them and make perfect looking bubbles.

Believe in your dreams

Size: 8" x 8"

Ariel and Friends

by Yvonne Verdonk

Supplies:

Epoxy Stickers: Ariel, Papers: Cinderella - Purple, Ariel Tonal, Extras: cardstock, distressing ink, colored staples, brads, fibres, paper clip, glitter

Tip:

Use a very fine line of clear drying glue to adhere the glitter on the title.

Ariel's Grotto
by Kathy Fesmire

Supplies:

Stickers: Little Mermaid, Little Mermaid Borders, Paper: Little Mermaid Corner, Extras: cardstock, micro beads, seashells, netting, foam squares, wire, fishing line, distressing ink, raffia

Tip:

Using the netting gives the sense of being "Under the Sea". Library cards make perfect tags.

Size: 12" x 12"

Sparkles like the sea

Size: 12" x 12"

Ariel
by Yvonne Verdonk

Supplies:

Stickers: Little Mermaid, Epoxy Stickers: Ariel, Rub-on Transfers: Ariel, Papers: Little Mermaid Image, Pooh Blue/Green, Ariel Tonal, Extras: cardstock, ribbon, staples, distressing ink

Tip:

The torn paper strips are glued along the top and bottom edges only. This creates a unique pocket to slide tags in and out of.

Belle

by Kathy Fesmire

Size: 8" x 8"

Supplies:

Stickers: Belle, Belle Borders, Paper: Belle Corner, Extras: cardstock, ribbon, distressing ink, eyelet, ribbon roses

Beautiful Belle

by Gigi Tung

Supplies:

Stickers: Belle, Princesses, Epoxy Stickers: Belle, Extras: cardstock, ribbon, distressing ink

Tip:

The bottom tag can hide a picture or secret journaling.

Meeting a Princess

Four is such a fun age to take your children to Disneyland Park. When we took Aysha there she believed in everything magical about the place. Meeting Belle was one of the highlights of the trip and Belle was wonderful with her. She spent lots of time talking to Aysha and even showed her how to curtsy like a real princess! Disneyland Park, September 1997

Belle

Meeting a Princess

by Trudy Sigurdson

Supplies:

Embossed Die-cuts: Belle, Extras: cardstock, foam squares

Tip:

Great layouts don't always require a lot of supplies!

Size: 12" x 12"

Maleficent

by Trudy Sigurdson

Size: 8" x 8"

Supplies:

Stickers: Disney Villains Female, Extras: cardstock, elasticized ribbon, distressing ink, foam squares

Cruella De Vil

by Trudy Sigurdson

Size: 8" x 8"

Supplies:

Stickers: Disney Villains Female,

Extras: cardstock, ribbon, distressing ink, foam squares

Villains

Mirror, Mirror, On the Wall…

by Yvonne Verdonk

Size: 8" x 8"

Supplies:

Stickers: Disney Villains Female, Jasmine Borders, Paper: Cinderella - Purple, Extras: cardstock, embossing powder

inspirations

The world of Disney is a place of imagination and inspiration. On these pages and sprinkled throughout this book, we have assembled a collection of phrases, titles, words and quotes that may inspire a page or add the perfect finishing touch.

Disney

Let the adventure begin

Magical moments

Wow! Friends are the things most worth celebrating

Disney friends

Where dreams **Fun!** really do come true

The happiest place on earth

Be our guest

Laughter   Let the magic begin

Imagination

Welcome to a world of dreams

Mickey and the Gang

In the mouse house

Hey Mickey! Let's play!

Mousin' around

Hugs from Mickey

Getting Goofy Quack attack

Gimme some glove

Forever sweethearts

Girls will be girls. Thank goodness!

Feeling flirty

No pals like old pals Adorable!

Well, whaddya know!

I'M ALL EARS

Make every moment count

How'd that happen?

Best buddies Smilers always win

The gang's all here

Goof Troop

Mouse Magic

Princesses

If the slipper fits, wear it

A kiss takes care of everything

Once upon a time starts with a gown

Princess in training

Magic beneath the sea

I wear the glass slippers in this house

Always dreaming

Littlest princess

Fairy Godmother, are you there?

Such a princess

Just like a princess

Once there was a princess

Fairy tales do come true

Pretty as a princess

Life is a ball

Simply splashy

Thank heavens for little princesses

Born to Rule

Once upon a fairy tale

Pooh and Friends

Oh, bother!

A togetherish sort of day

Tiggers are a wonderful thing

Might be coming. Might be going.

Don't be afraid to bee you

Splendiferous

Deep in the Hundred Acre Wood

Huglet, snuglet, cute-as-a-buglet

Bounce outside the lines

Don't let my size fool you

Can't bee bothered

Forget your bothers

Willy, nilly, silly old bear

Bounce or get bounced!

Don't do. Bee.

Tiggerific

> "It's kind of fun to do the impossible"
>
> -Walt Disney

Products

Stickers

Papers

Rub-on Transfers

Epoxy Stickers

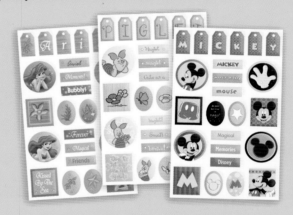

Embossed Stickers

Embossed Die-cuts

A Magical Dream

by Beth Leonard

Size: 8" x 8"

Supplies:

Stickers: Princess Phrases, Sleeping Beauty, Papers: Sleeping Beauty Left, Sleeping Beauty Right, Cinderella - Pink, Extras: cardstock, ribbon, glitter, star brads, tulle

Tip:

Tulle has a wonderful quality to soften and add texture to layouts. Tulle is attached to the back of the layout and gathered on the front with a bow.

Size: 12" x 12"

Believe in happy endings

Sleeping Beauty

by Trudy Sigurdson

Supplies:

Stickers: Sleeping Beauty, Sleeping Beauty Borders, Papers: Sleeping Beauty Right, Extras: cardstock, cotton lace, paper flowers, foam squares

Tip:

You can never have enough journaling to remember the moment.

Aysha has been to Disneyland Park twice, once when she was 4 years old and now at 11. The first time we went she HAD to go see all of the Princesses, every single one of them. I would stand with her in the line ups for hours so she could meet Cinderella, Snow White, Belle and the others. However, the one Princess that she never got to see was Sleeping Beauty. When we went back there again in 2003, she was more interested in seeing other characters like Mickey Mouse and Winnie the Pooh and having her photo taken with them. So this year, the hunt for Princesses was not necessary. Good, we could line up for the RIDES this time! On the day we were due to fly home, we decided we wanted to sneak in 2 more hours at the park before having to leave for the airport. We were there nice and early and were in the line up for the front gates to open. When we walked into the park and towards Main St. USA, we noticed that just to the left by the Disneyland Bank, Sleeping Beauty was standing there all by herself. Now I don't know if it was because there was no line ups or because she didn't see her on our last trip, but Aysha really wanted to meet her and have her photo taken. Alex on the other hand was quite content to pass up this photo-op and just look from a far. Disneyland Park, December 2003

Jasmine Card and Tag
by Cheryl Souter

Supplies - Card:
Stickers: Jasmine, Paper: Jasmine Corner, Extras: cardstock, vellum, eyelets, string, ribbon, distressing ink

Supplies - Tag:
Stickers: Princess Snapshots, Jasmine, Jasmine Borders, Paper: Jasmine Corner, Extras: cardstock, slide mount, embossed labels, ribbon, brads, safety pin, charm, eyelet, distressing ink

Tip:
After cutting out the frame for the card, the paper was crinkled and orange and teal ink was lightly run over the wrinkles to make them more defined.

The world's my magic carpet

Jasmine

Size: 12" x 12"

Princess Julia
by Gigi Tung

Supplies:
Stickers: Jasmine, Paper: Jasmine Corner, Extras: cardstock, vellum, brads, ribbon, photo mounts

Tip:
Slide mounts make great embellishments. Use them as frames or cover them for unique visual interest.

44

Tinker Bell

by Beth Leonard and Yvonne Verdonk

Supplies:

Stickers: Tinker Bell, Papers: Tinker Bell Tonal, Cinderella - Pink, Cinderella - Purple, Minnie Friendship - Green Patterned, Extras: cardstock, vellum, foam squares

Tip:

Cut out a like image of Tinker Bell from a second sheet of paper and place on top of the first (slightly offset) using foam squares to create a dimensional effect.

Perfect little flirt

Pretty Little Pixie

by Gigi Tung

Supplies:

Bits of Glitz Stickers: Tinker Bell, Epoxy Stickers: Tinker Bell, Paper: Tinker Bell Tonal, Extras: cardstock, ribbon, brad, distressing ink

We 'Tink' You're Beautiful

by Shannon Lavigne

Supplies:

Stickers: Tinker Bell, Tinker Bell Borders, Paper: Minnie Friendship - Green Patterned, Extras: cardstock, vellum, brads, micro beads, dimensional glaze

Tip:

There are many opportunities for a cute play on words.

My Autograph Book
by Shannon Lavigne

Supplies:

Stickers: Princess Snapshots, Papers: Cinderella - Pink, Cinderella - Purple, Travel - Clouds, Extras: cardstock, vellum, ribbon, brads, elasticized ribbon

Tip:

Cut the cover and inside pages to 4 3/4" x 12". Each piece will be layered one on top of the other with the binding running through the middle of the book using elasticized ribbon.

Smiles, love and kindness are royal riches

Size: 12" x 12"

Mommy's Little Princess
by Gigi Tung

Supplies:

Stickers: Princesses, Princess Phrases, Epoxy Stickers: Tinker Bell, Bits of Glitz Stickers: Cinderella, Tinker Bell, Paper: Cinderella - Pink, Extras: cardstock, ribbon, foam squares

Tip:

Layer stickers to create an interesting grouping as was done with the Princesses.

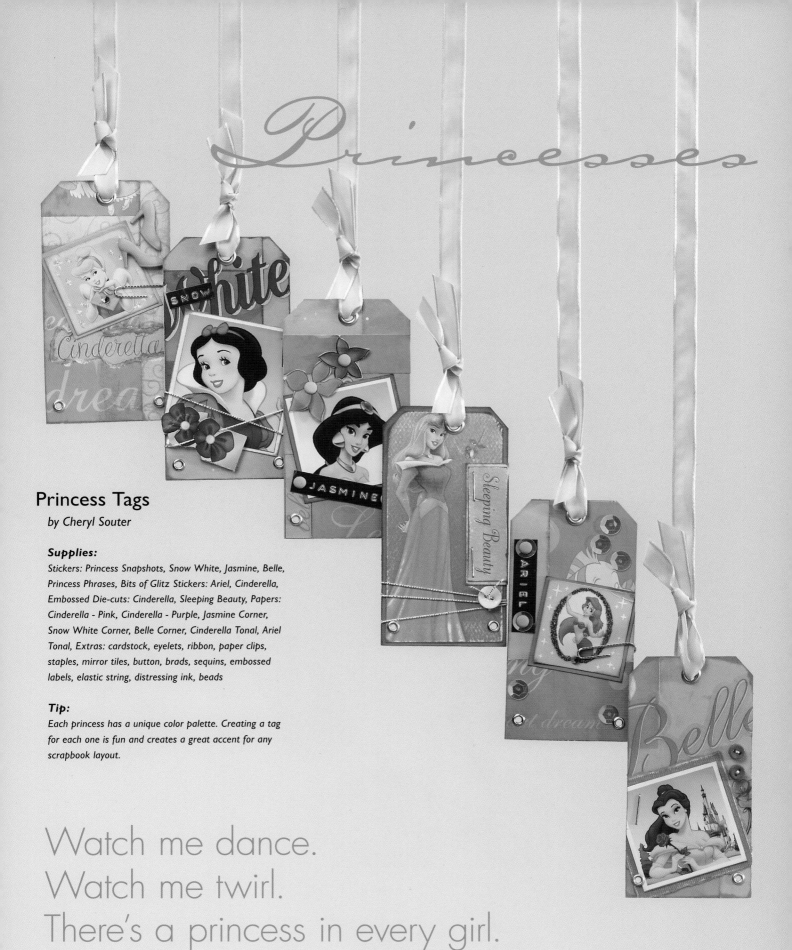

Princess Tags

by Cheryl Souter

Supplies:

Stickers: Princess Snapshots, Snow White, Jasmine, Belle, Princess Phrases, Bits of Glitz Stickers: Ariel, Cinderella, Embossed Die-cuts: Cinderella, Sleeping Beauty, Papers: Cinderella - Pink, Cinderella - Purple, Jasmine Corner, Snow White Corner, Belle Corner, Cinderella Tonal, Ariel Tonal, Extras: cardstock, eyelets, ribbon, paper clips, staples, mirror tiles, button, brads, sequins, embossed labels, elastic string, distressing ink, beads

Tip:

Each princess has a unique color palette. Creating a tag for each one is fun and creates a great accent for any scrapbook layout.

Watch me dance.
Watch me twirl.
There's a princess in every girl.

$\mathscr{Pooh}$ and Friends

Winnie the Pooh, the lovable bear who's stuffed with fluff, is also called Pooh or Pooh Bear, but never, ever, just Winnie.

Pooh endlessly craves a smackeral of whatever little something is at hand (preferably honey) to soothe that insatiable "rumbly in his tumbly."

But even honey isn't as important as his friends. Their happiness and feelings are Pooh's chief concern, and there is no better friend than Winnie the Pooh.

Tigger
Impulsive
Fun-loving
Care-free
Adventurous

Piglet
Curious
Considerate
Timid
Insecure

Eeyore
Generous
Intelligent
Quiet
Gloomy

Size: 8" x 8"

Winnie the Pooh
by Cheryl Souter

Supplies:
Stickers: Pooh Phrases, Epoxy Stickers: Pooh, Papers: Pooh, Bees & Honey, Pooh Name, Extras: cardstock, ribbon, eyelets, brads, ticket stubs

Tip:
For the random letters in the word 'hundred', cut apart the words on the Pooh Phrase Sheet.

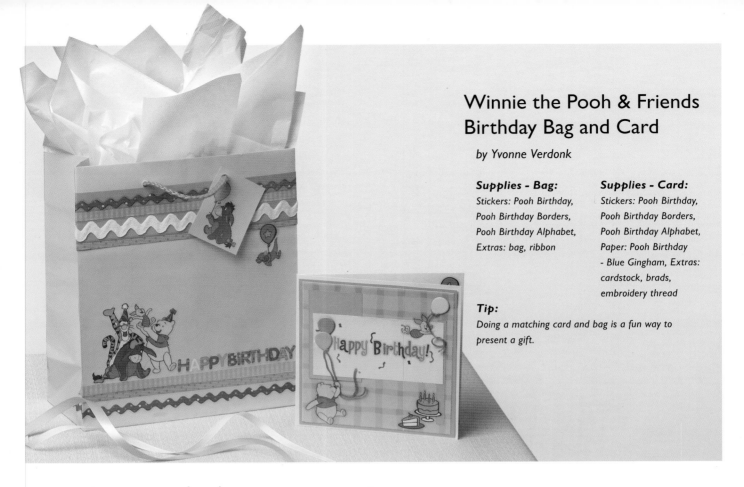

Winnie the Pooh & Friends Birthday Bag and Card

by Yvonne Verdonk

Supplies - Bag:
Stickers: Pooh Birthday, Pooh Birthday Borders, Pooh Birthday Alphabet, Extras: bag, ribbon

Supplies - Card:
Stickers: Pooh Birthday, Pooh Birthday Borders, Pooh Birthday Alphabet, Paper: Pooh Birthday - Blue Gingham, Extras: cardstock, brads, embroidery thread

Tip:
Doing a matching card and bag is a fun way to present a gift.

Happy Birthday to you!

Size: 12" x 12"

Lil' Miss Allie

by Yvonne Verdonk

Supplies:
Stickers: Pooh Birthday, Pooh Birthday Borders, Pooh Birthday Alphabet, Papers: Pooh Birthday - Blue Gingham, Pooh Birthday - Yellow Patterned, Extras: cardstock, ribbon

Tip:
Tags are inset into pockets hiding more photos of the party. A great way to use more pictures.

Winnie the Pooh

by Angela Brock

Supplies:

Embossed Die-cuts: Pooh, Papers: Pooh - Blue/Green, Pooh - Yellow Stripe, Bees & Honey, Extras: cardstock, slide mount, rick rack, ribbon, flower brads, foam squares, raffia

Size: 12" x 12"

A good friend, indeed!

It's So Much Friendlier with Pooh

by Kathy Fesmire

Supplies:

Frame Kit: Pooh, Bits of Glitz Stickers: Pooh, Paper: Bees & Honey, Extras: cardstock, vellum, ribbon, eyelets, distressing ink, brads, foam squares

Every Child loves Winnie the Pooh! The kids couldn't wait to find him to have their picture taken with him. We found him with Tigger and Piglet at Disney's Animal Kingdom Theme Park by the docks. He was just as sweet in person as he is in the book we've read and movies we've seen.

Size: 8" x 8"

Bounce On Over
Tigger Card
by Shannon Lavigne

Supplies:
*Stickers: Tigger, Paper: Stripes,
Tigger Name, Extras: cardstock,
cardboard, vellum*

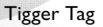

Tigger Tag
by Shannon Lavigne

Supplies:
*Rub-on Transfers: Tigger, Embossed
Die-cuts: Tigger, Paper: Pooh - Yellow
Stripe, Tigger Name, Extras: cardstock,
ribbon, brad, eyelet, distressing ink*

Tip:
*Rub-ons can be placed over
multiple layers of paper.*

Tiggers are
wonderful
things

Tigger
by Trudy Sigurdson

Supplies:
*Embossed Stickers: Tigger, Tigger
Borders, Paper: Tigger Stripes,
Extras: cardstock, buttons*

Aysha, Alex and Trudy with Tigger
Pooh's Corner, Disneyland Park
December 2003

Size: 12" x 12"

Tigger Gift Bag

by Yvonne Verdonk

Supplies:

*Stickers: Tigger, Pooh Phrases, Puffy Fuzzy
Stickers: Tigger, Embossed Die-cuts: Tigger,
Papers: Tigger Tonal, Tigger Name, Extras:
cardstock, embroidery thread*

Tip:

*The tag pops out of the bottom of the bag.
A great gift giving idea.*

TTFN - Ta ta for now

Size: 12" x 12"

Tigger Balloon

*by Beth Leonard
and Yvonne Verdonk*

Supplies:

*Stickers: Tigger, Tigger Borders, Pooh Alphabet - Orange, Pooh Phrases, Epoxy
Stickers: Tigger, Embossed Die-cuts: Tigger, Bits of Glitz Stickers: Tigger,
Papers: Mickey Travel - Clouds, Tigger Stripes, Tigger Tonal, Tigger Name,
Extras: cardstock, embroidery thread, brads, jump rings, foam squares*

Tip:

*Creative paper piecing projects using patterned
papers, fibres and jump rings add fun and interest.*

Mikayla has always loved Piglet, in fact she would always call herself "Pigget" (she couldn't say Piglet properly at the time). So she was so excited when she actually got to see Piglet at Disneyland Park. We were walking near Main St. USA and Piglet was just standing there all by himself. Mikayla went running up to him and gave him a hug, but when she was ready to leave, Piglet was not ready to let her go and just kept right on hugging her. Luckily she didn't mind too much!
November 1999

sweet things come in small packages

Size: 12" x 12"

Piglet

by Trudy Sigurdson

Supplies:

Stickers: Piglet, Piglet Borders, Paper: Piglet Tonal, Extras: cardstock, lace, foam squares

Don't let my size fool you

Piglet Frame and Card
by Shannon Lavigne

Supplies - Frame:
Stickers: Piglet, Paper:
Piglet Tonal, Extras: ribbon,
watchmaker tag, epoxy
dome sticker, foam squares

Supplies - Card:
Stickers: Piglet, Epoxy
Stickers: Piglet, Paper:
Piglet Tonal, Extras:
cardstock, ribbon, foam
squares

Tip:
A frame covered with Piglet paper makes the perfect
frame for a new baby. A 3D cut-out of Piglet from the
paper is placed on the bottom left corner. Some ribbon,
an initial and stickers complete this simple project.

Piglet Tag
by Shannon Lavigne

Supplies:
Stickers: Pooh Snapshots, Piglet,
Epoxy Stickers: Piglet, Frame Kit:
Piglet, Papers: Pooh - Blue/Green,
Piglet Tonal, Extras: cardstock,
jump rings, ribbon, foam squares

Tip:
Jump rings are used to hang the
Piglet epoxy letters from the
bottom of the tag.

Little me,
shy as can be

Messages from Piglet
by Gigi Tung

Supplies:
Stickers: Piglet, Rub-on Transfers:
Piglet, Paper: Piglet Tonal, Extras:
cardstock, matchboxes, ribbon, beads,
string, foam squares, distressing ink

Tip:
You can hide special messages or small
gifts inside the matchboxes.

Shy and sweet

Think Cheery
by Shannon Lavigne

Supplies - Tag:
Stickers: Pooh Snapshots, Paper: Pooh - Blue/Green, Extras: cardstock, slide mount, eyelet, ribbon, foam squares

Supplies - Card:
Stickers: Eeyore, Paper: Pooh - Blue/Green, Extras: cardstock, ribbon, brads, foam squares, micro beads

Tip:
Mat the flowers on paper, sand them, cut them out and attach them to the card with foam squares. Add brads to the center of the two smaller flowers and micro beads to the center of the large flower.

Thanks for noticing me

Eeyore
by Trudy Sigurdson

Supplies:
Stickers: Eeyore, Eeyore Borders, Extras: cardstock, eyelets, string, foam squares

Tip:
Hang your title from eyelets giving it a feeling of being suspended under the picture.

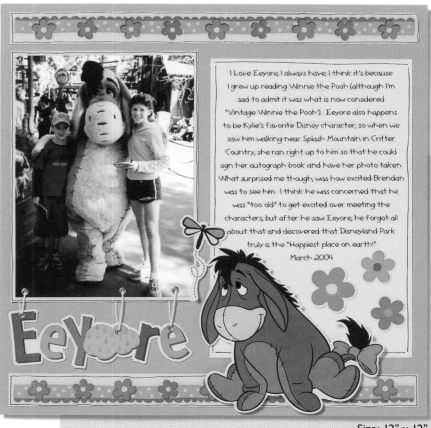

I Love Eeyore, I always have, I think it's because I grew up reading Winnie the Pooh (although I'm sad to admit it was what is now considered "Vintage Winnie the Pooh"). Eeyore also happens to be Kylie's favorite Disney character, so when we saw him walking near Splash Mountain in Critter Country, she ran right up to him so that he could sign her autograph book and have her photo taken. What surprised me though, was how excited Brendan was to see him. I think he was concerned that he was "too old" to get excited over meeting the characters, but after he saw Eeyore, he forgot all about that and discovered that Disneyland Park truly is the "Happiest place on earth!"
March 2004

Size: 12" x 12"

Friends

We'll be friends forever, wait and see

Pooh-isms

by Cheryl Souter

Supplies:

*Stickers: Pooh Snapshots, Pooh Phrases, Embossed Die-cuts: Tigger,
Papers: Pooh - Yellow Stripe, Pooh Poses, Winnie the Pooh Tonal, Tigger
Tonal, Piglet Tonal, Extras: cardstock, brads, washers, embossed label,
distressing ink, ribbon, rub-on numbers*

Tip:

*The tag pulls out of the holder to reveal the
Pooh-isms, or secret journaling.*

Cuddly friend

Me and Winnie the Pooh

by Gigi Tung

Size: 8" x 8"

Supplies:
Stickers: Pooh Snapshots, Pooh Phrases, Epoxy Stickers: Tigger, Papers: Winnie the Pooh Tonal, Tigger Tonal, Extras: cardstock, ribbon, foam squares

oh bother | friendly | sunny | 100 | acre | woods | cheery | dreams | hooray! | special | friendship | cuddly | stuffed | Tigger | bear

Pooh and his friends Piglet, Eeyore and Tigger, are amongst our favorite Disney characters and ones we always seek out for photo ops at the park. On our first day we went to Disney's Animal Kingdom Theme Park and saw that Tigger and Eeyore were having a meet n' greet and signing autographs. Aysha and Alex both wanted to go and meet them. While they were doing this, I asked their helper if Piglet was around, (up until this trip we had never seen Piglet and didn't know if he lived at the park). She told us that he, along with the yellow rabbit, were a bit elusive and didn't make too many appearances, but to go to one of the stores and they could phone the "Chip Hotline" and could then find out if he would be out and about. No luck. He was not going to be out that day or the next, Wednesday. Apparently, Piglet always plays golf on Wednesdays. So, we enjoyed seeing Eeyore and Tigger while we had the chance, and went off to explore the rest of the park. I love parades, especially Disney parades and always try to see all of them if I can. On our last day the only parade I had yet to see was the "Share a Dream Come True" parade. No one else wanted to see it, not even Aysha. They all wanted to go ride on "The Pirates of the Caribbean". Although I loved that ride, I had been on it many times and I had never seen this parade (plus I'm a scrapper and want the photos!). So, I stood in place along the curb waiting for the parade while everyone else went o the rides. I'm so glad I did. Not only did I see Pooh (who I hadn't seen yet on this trip), but I also saw Piglet walking around with his kite.
Walt Disney World Resort 2004

Winnie the Pooh and Friends

by Trudy Sigurdson

Size: 12" x 12"

Supplies:
Stickers: Pooh Snapshots, Pooh Phrases, Pooh, Pooh Borders, Pooh Alphabet - Orange, Paper: Pooh - Yellow Stripe, Extras: cardstock, foam squares

Tip:
Layering "Pooh" words across two pages gives the eye a place to go.

Winnie the Pooh Case
by Yvonne Verdonk

Supplies:
Stickers: Pooh Sketchbook, Pooh Phrases, Rub-on Transfers: Pooh & Friends, Extras: mini lunch box, paint, cardstock, beaded chain, heart charm, distressing ink

Tip:
A mini tin lunch box was lightly sanded, primed and painted with quick drying matte paint. Distressing ink is applied on the corners and edges to coordinate with the Pooh stickers. Rub-ons and stickers adhere perfectly to the paint.

I wonder what I'll wonder next

Sketchbook Mini Book
by Shannon Lavigne

Supplies:
Stickers: Pooh Sketchbook, Papers: Pooh Name, Tigger Tonal, Extras: cardstock, ribbon, eyelet, distressing ink

While we were walking around Downtown Disney we decided to check out the huge Disney store that is there. At the back of the store were huge piles of stuffed Disney characters. Straight away Aysha was drawn to a pile of Poohs and not being one to miss a photo opportunity, I asked her to sit amongst them all and give one a big hug.
Disneyland Park, December 2003

Winnie the Pooh and Friends

by Trudy Sigurdson

Supplies:
Stickers: Pooh Sketchbook, Papers: Pooh - Yellow Stripe, Pooh Name, Extras: cardstock, rub-ons, ribbon, buttons, foam squares, distressing ink

Tip:
By inking the edges of the paper the distressed look has taken down the tone of the paper and stickers giving it the look of "Hunny".

Size: 12" x 12"

Nothing warms the heart like friendship

Hum dee dum, friends are fun

The Gang

by Shannon Lavigne

Supplies:
Stickers: Pooh Sketchbook, Papers: Tigger Name, Pooh Name, Extras: cardstock, vellum, brads

Tip:
A mix of kids, a mix of papers. Don't be afraid to mix your favorites!

These three are such a bunch of goofs! They've known each other almost all their lives. They love to spend time playing all different games. Now that we live so far from each other, these pictures are all the more special. This Easter day was a fun one for all of us. This is our gang. Always.

Kaeden, Alyssa and Sterling
Easter Sunday 2003

Size: 12" x 12"

Waiting for Baby

by Shannon Lavigne

Supplies:

Stickers: Pooh Watercolor, Pooh Watercolor Accents, Papers: Colorful Squares, Tonal Squares, Little Thoughts, Tonal Dots, Balloons, Honey Pots, Extras: cardboard, cardstock, vellum, foam squares, brads, eyelets, fibres, ribbon, binder rings

Tip:

The Pooh Watercolor collection is perfect for babies.

Shiny and new
and so tiny, too

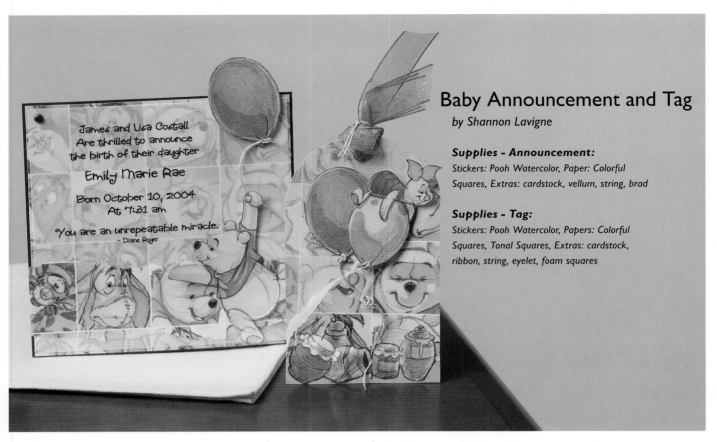

Baby Announcement and Tag
by Shannon Lavigne

Supplies - Announcement:
Stickers: Pooh Watercolor, Paper: Colorful Squares, Extras: cardstock, vellum, string, brad

Supplies - Tag:
Stickers: Pooh Watercolor, Papers: Colorful Squares, Tonal Squares, Extras: cardstock, ribbon, string, eyelet, foam squares

James and Lisa Costall Are thrilled to announce the birth of their daughter

Emily Marie Rae

Born October 10, 2004 At 7:31 am

You are an unrepeatable miracle.
– Diane Roger

My little cuddle bear

Size: 8" x 8"

A Boy and His Bear
by Shannon Lavigne

Supplies:
Papers: Little Thoughts, Tonal Dots, Honey Pots, Extras: cardstock, ribbon, rubber stamps, string, foam squares

Tip:
Layer a second Pooh Bear over the original Pooh on the paper to create a dimensional effect.

Friends Tag
by Cheryl Souter

Supplies:
Stickers: Pooh Watercolor, Pooh Watercolor Accents, Paper: Colorful Squares, Extras: cardstock, ribbon, photo mount, brads, eyelet, embossed vellum, foam squares, distressing ink

Tip:
Stitching is a great effect that pulls all elements of the tag together.

Carefree

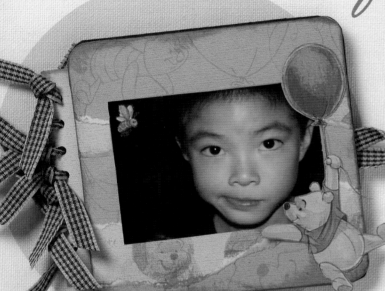

Winnie the Pooh Pocket Book

by Gigi Tung

Supplies:

Stickers: Pooh Phrases, Pooh Watercolor Accents, Rub-on Transfers: Pooh & Friends, Papers: Balloons, Tonal Dots, Little Thoughts, Extras: cardboard, cardstock, ribbon, brads

Thinking little thoughts of you

Size: 12" x 12"

Dreaming

by Cheryl Souter

Supplies:

Stickers: Pooh Watercolor, Papers: Colorful Squares, Tonal Squares, Little Thoughts, Extras: cardstock, printable fabric, vellum, string, distressing ink, brads, prong steel fastener, foam squares

Tip:

After printing the picture on printable fabric, the backing was peeled off so that the cotton fabric could be torn and the edges frayed before sewing it onto the mat.

Classics

Every night, just before the lights go out, children run to the bookshelf and pull out their favorite story book. There is no question that countless bedtimes have been made special by the reading of a treasured Disney Classic story.

The Disney Classics include many of the world's favorite characters and story lines. From Dumbo and his tale of courage and triumph to Cruella de Vil and her ruthless and cold-hearted antics, the Classics deliver powerful messages which are both inspirational and timeless.

Chip and Dale
Scheming

Captain Hook
Flamboyant
Disreputable
Malevolent
Obsessive

Maleficent
Pure evil

Cruella De Vil
Sophisticated
Erratic
Ruthless

Going to Disneyland Park with a "cool" teenager is not the easiest of things to do, especially if you are a scrapbooker and are wanting to take photos. Tiffany did not want her photo taken... and most definitely not with any characters. That would be "so lame!" So we ended up learning how to compromise. That meant that I would be allowed to take a few pictures and the characters could be bronze ones that are at the end of Main St. USA around the Walt Disney and Mickey Mouse statue. That was fine by me... I wanted photos of those anyway! Disneyland Park July 2003

Size: 12" x 12"

Dumbo and Tiffany

by Trudy Sigurdson

Supplies:

Stickers: Dumbo, Dumbo Borders, Paper: Dumbo Stripes, Extras: cardstock, ribbon, distressing ink, foam squares

Chip & Dale

by Trudy Sigurdson

Supplies:

Stickers: Chip & Dale, Extras: cardstock, tags, twine, brads, distressing ink

Tip:

The tree was created by using strips of cardstock and ink.

Size: 8" x 8"

Size: 8" x 8"

The plank awaits!

Captain Hook

by Trudy Sigurdson

Supplies:

Stickers: Disney Villains Male, Extras: cardstock, ribbon, brads, glitter, distressing ink

Tip:

By adding glitter to the title, you add dimension to the page.

Jafar

by Trudy Sigurdson

Supplies:

Stickers: Disney Villains Male, Extras: cardstock, ribbon, distressing ink, foam squares

So many curses, so little time

Size: 8" x 8"

Puffy Fuzzy Stickers

Bits of Glitz Stickers

Frame Kits

Memory Page Frames

8x8 Scrapbook Albums

12x12 Scrapbook Albums

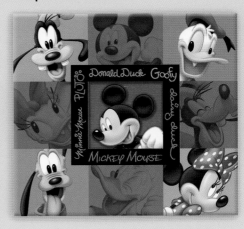

*To view Sandylion's complete Disney Scrapbook Collection, visit **www.sandylion.com***

Contributors

Shannon　　Trudy　　Gigi　　Kathy　　Cheryl　　Beth　　Yvonne

Shannon Lavigne

As an avid scrapbooker who has worked in the industry since 1998, I currently design and teach full time in this wonderful world of paper and stickers. This is my dream job. With two gorgeous sons and a wonderful husband, I am never short of inspiration. Whether it be taking the photos that will end up on the pages or dreaming up new and creative ways to use different products, working for Sandylion gives me the opportunity to create and educate - and for me, there's nothing better than that.

Trudy Sigurdson

Trudy currently resides in Victoria, B.C., Canada, but is originally from England. Though her background is in graphic design and fine arts, it was her introduction to scrapbooking that soon put her on the fast track to turning a hobby into a full-time passion. In September 2002, her creativity won her a coveted position as one of the original 10 Memory Makers' Masters and ever since her work has been featured regularly in Memory Makers magazines and various other magazines such as Creating Keepsakes, Simple Scrapbooks, Scrapbook Retailer, Country Marketplace and Arts & Crafts Canada. Trudy is an avid photographer (whose favorite subjects are her two children, Aysha and Alex) and is always looking for new and innovative ways to create her own one-of-a-kind layouts.

Gigi Tung

I have always been a creative person, from studying visual arts to owning my own scrapbook store. Sandylion introduced me to scrapbooking and has helped fuel my passion for this wonderful art form. Scrapbooking is a rewarding hobby that has made me realize how important it is to take the time to explore all that life has to offer and make every moment a truly special one.

Kathy Fesmire

I am a stay at home mom to four children and spend what little spare time I have teaching art, freelancing and scrapbooking just for the joy of it. In addition, I coordinate all day scrapbooking events. I started scrapbooking in 1997 and have loved watching the craft grow and evolve. I was honored to be named a Memory Makers Master in 2004 and enjoy teaching scrapbooking classes on various subjects at scrapbook stores, events and trade shows. Luckily, I have a wonderful, supportive husband who is very understanding of just how addictive this hobby is!

Cheryl Souter

My main reason for scrapbooking has always been my family. I have three terrific children and a wonderful husband who always supports me and my scrapbook addiction. I started working in the industry in 1999 to support my habit and have branched into design work for products, magazines, local store displays, and advertising. I am truly excited to have been asked to be a part of the Sandylion team and look forward to my next creative challenges.

Beth Leonard

I have been a part of the scrapbook scene since 1998. The knowledge I have gained this far is truly priceless. I have worked at a local scrapbook store where I have taught numerous classes and have also lectured at trade shows. I love the challenge that fun paper, stickers and pictures present. I hope that the Disney layouts that I have created in this book serve as a wonderful source of inspiration.

Yvonne Verdonk

Scrapbooking is a hobby that brings together my loves and interests: family, photography and history with color, design and texture. As a wife and as the mother of five busy sons, I have constant inspiration for my next scrapbook project. I enjoy sharing my love of scrapbooking as a retailer, teacher, designer and consultant.

Note from the editors:

It has been our dream to create a book filled with inspiring projects using Sandylion's wonderful Disney themed scrapbook collections. We brought together an exceptional design team whose diversity and creativity have made this book truly magical. We hope that this book will inspire endless ideas that bring your family and your favorite Disney characters together in memorable and meaningful ways.

Debora Sakala　　Nancy Duckman